FACES OF WISDOM

Elders of the World

ETHAN HUBBARD

Harry Smith and Daniel Von Trapp
Waitsfield, Vermont,
USA

PREFACE

In the spring of 1978, nearing my 38th year and determined to bring a deeper sense of fulfillment into my life, I sold my house and land in northern Vermont and began spending as much time as possible with rural and indigenous people.

For the previous ten years, I had worked as the deputy director of the Vermont Historical Society, collecting and preserving artifacts for the Vermont Museum and Library. Whenever I felt overwhelmed by my desk work, I checked out of the office with a couple of cameras and a tape recorder and would visit with interesting Vermonters: blacksmiths, loggers, farmers, homesteaders, and especially the elders whose life stories brought me no end of pleasure. Soon, I realized that interviewing and photographing people was what I wanted to do with my life, so I quit my job at the Historical Society and embarked upon travel. My first real adventure was a two-year ramble around the United States in an old VW camper, complete with cameras and my dog, Willow.

It was not, as I now look back upon it, a sense of disillusionment with being a householder that prompted me to travel as much as some inner need seeking alignment with simple and natural things: growing seeds, harvesting food, sleeping on the earth by a river, listening to the wind in the trees, and sitting on porches with wise elders wiling away a summer's afternoon.

Between 1978 and 1980, I drove the back roads of America, stopping to visit with interesting people who were leading lives very different from mine. The Native Americans especially interested me — the Navajos, Apaches, Papagos, and Sioux. I traveled to their reservations in my VW bus, with camping gear stashed beneath the bed. I always managed to find an elder who seemed happy to have me about. I would sit at his feet and ask questions from my heart, and visits flowed from minutes into days of sharing.

It was an America I had forgotten existed — a land of wide open spaces to set your mind free, of tiny prairie villages with welcoming cafes, church socials, and friendly people enjoying good talk on the streets. I shared coffee with cowboys in Wyoming, danced with Cajun rice harvesters in Louisiana, herded cattle with Idaho school children, and brought in winter wood with Southerners and their mules.

In 1980, I began traveling farther afield: the Outer Hebrides of Scotland, Mexico's Sierra Madre, Guatemala's jungles, the mountains of Nepal, India's Ladakh region, Australia, New Zealand, Indonesia, the Caribbean, Greece, Egypt, and Sri Lanka. Long trips included six months in an Incan village in the Andes of Peru, and a full year of traipsing after shepherds in England and Wales.

I traveled as simply and economically as I could, with a knapsack, a tent, light cooking gear, cameras, film, and small gifts to give to people who befriended me along the way.

Each country was alluring in its own way. The mountains and deserts, the high steppes and tundra, the islands and moors and the rainforest jungles all awakened in me a deep sense of appreciation and a fuller understanding of my life. The different cultures proved to be empowering teachers, too. Each village and family reflected ways of living that were new to me. The Nepalese, for example, could grow a year's supply of food on a plot of ground not much bigger than a house. The Inuits, who often gave their babies away to barren families, taught unconditional love. The Native Americans held a reverence for the natural world. The Maoris knew the joy of singing. The Australian Aborigines believed that dreams were more real than the ordinary world. The Scots had learned to accept the weather, the Tibetans, their fate. The Mexicans loved laughter and practical jokes.

Perhaps as much as anything, my association with elders became paramount. I sought them out with a keen determination. Their ways fascinated me: their wisdom, their integrity, their relationship with themselves and with fellow human beings. I took great pains to watch everything they did and said, how they built fires, made bread, fished, hunted, worked with animals, held children, laughed, cried. I marveled at how they would rise with a smile upon their faces and turn to sleep each night with a look of thankfulness etched upon their countenance. The wisdom of their lives was reflected from those faces and captured by these photographs. This book — their lives — is a gift returned to them and to you, the reader.

Ethan Hubbard
Washington, Connecticut
1993

Epimanuel Valdez
Penitente Elder from Colorado,
USA

INTRODUCTION

by Julia Tavares de Alvarez

Ambassador to the United Nations from The Dominican Republic

Some time ago, I received a postcard from my daughter, Julia. On it was an image that compelled my attention. It was a photograph, shot from behind, of an elderly peasant couple holding hands. I could not take my eyes off it, and the simple picture sent my mind reeling.

Although the people were slightly bent, they seemed to exude life and energy. It was also clear that this couple loved and cared for each other. Their body language spoke volumes about that.

On the card, my daughter had written something that at first seemed startling but then made a great deal of sense. The couple in the picture had reminded her of her parents. The reason I was initially surprised was that at first glance the clearly peasant clothing that the couple in the photograph wore hardly reflected the life my husband Eduardo and I, both professionals, lead. But looking at the image for more than a second or two quickly established that as a secondary, surface characteristic. And I was touched and moved that Julia would see the affection and support offered each other by these two older people as a reminder of us.

The Silvas
San Miguel de Allende,
Mexico

Who were these people who seemed so bound together? A photographer had once told me that pictures of people express emotion through their eyes, hands, and mouths. Yet here was a photo that hid all that except for the slightest glimpse of part of their joined hands.

The couple seemed to be very much striding forward — toward what? I conjured up a life for them. I imagined, through the years, their joys and sorrow: children raised to adulthood, perhaps a farm worked until hard physical labor was no longer practical. And now, what?

What did old age mean to them? What did it have to offer? Were they part of some community that acknowledges the value of their lives, their contributions to the common life of all — now, for what they might still do, as well as for the life they had lived so far? Did society still care about and need them? Or were they already part of history and nothing else? Did they have only each other, and outside of that, isolation?

All this just from a photograph in which their faces were not even visible.

I knew I had to meet the photographer whose work could affect me so strongly. On the back of the card I found the address of the Chelsea Green Publishing Company, and through them I was able to get in touch with Ethan Hubbard.

I was not surprised to find that Ethan is a man who marches to the beat of his own drum. People gifted with imagination and empathy for those not like themselves often stride off the beaten path, for that is where one may gain some perspective on life: looking from the outside in.

Not that Ethan is an "oddball." On the contrary, he is a man filled with common sense in the best meaning of both words. He also is a person with a common touch, to which his photographs of older people so eloquently testify.

Faces of Wisdom: Elders of the World is a book of Ethan's photographs of people who represent an important and far too neglected part of society. While elders, like any group, share some characteristics especially their own, they are still very much a part of our communities — if we will permit them to play a full role in them.

Ethan's pictures honor the subjects by accepting them on their own terms. These are not images of people whom the photographer had made colorful, eccentric, comic or preciously cute. Instead, they show aging naked on the human face. They are us some time down the road — if we are lucky.

This book is not a dirge for times past. It is a celebration of what older people are and might be. *Faces of Wisdom* is about people who are needed as well as loved. Thus, there are chapters about work, the family and intergenerational relationships. In my own work, as ambassador to the United Nations from the Dominican Republic, I, too, try to convey the worth and value of older people. It is the subject of aging, especially as it manifests itself in our Third World, which I have taken for my special concern.

This I know: We must begin to see older persons as serious, functioning members of society. Becoming sentimental about them or ignoring them is a luxury we cannot afford. By the turn of the century, especially in our developing nations, they will be making up an increasingly larger percentage of all populations against a backdrop of economies that will still be struggling to provide the bare necessities of life to people of all ages.

Ethan Hubbard's images of older people compel our respect for them as well as provide us with delight and aesthetic satisfaction. It is an attitude that society needs to cultivate, because before too long, if we have any sense, we will be looking to elders to contribute to the solutions of society's problems.

It is good to have a person like Ethan as a comrade in the struggle to bring elders back into "the family of man." But to be honest, since I work with the written and spoken word, I am not quite ready to concede that just one of Ethan's pictures is worth as many as a thousand of my own words. Nevertheless, the rate of exchange is clearly in his favor.

In the hard fight to make manifest the humanity and value of older people, I found Ethan Hubbard an important and powerful ally. More than that, I love his photographs and am now proud to call him my friend.

Julia Tavares de Alvarez
New York, 1993

FAMILY

Over the years, I have often forsaken the comfort and privacy of a good hostelry in favor of a home stay with a family. I am inexplicably drawn to certain houses, vaguely intuiting that within their walls lie things I wish to discover or reclaim. I stand nervously knocking at the door, my backpack upon my back, trying to keep my too-long hair from blowing about, making myself presentable. More often than not, I do not know exactly what it is I am going to say when the door opens. I only know that I am willing to open myself up to the possibility of something happening for the good. The door opens, and an elderly woman stares out at me, a slight beatific smile on her face. "Can I help you?" she asks politely. I find myself blurting out something. "Hello, my name is Ethan. I've come from a long ways away. I would like to spend time in your village. Is there a chance I could put up my tent somewhere out of the way, perhaps down in your woods?" And ninety-nine times out of a hundred, the person will nod her head affirmatively, smiling. "Yes, we're happy to have a guest about. It's fine for you to stay. Put your backpack here in the corner. You'll find a good tenting place down along the fence line near the forest. And be sure to come back for a meal with us. We'll be eating just after sundown."

Elroy Chase and Father, Albert
Middlesex, Vermont,
USA

Cajun "Treator" and Wife
Louisiana,
USA

The Silvas, Married 57 Years
San Miguel de Allende,
Mexico

Estratia and Helene, Sisters
Isle of Lesvos,
Greece

The MacCormicks
Outer Hebrides,
Scotland

Father and Son Cutting Wood
Along the Haitian Border,
The Dominican Republic

Father and Daughter
The Dominican Republic

Grandparents and Grandson
Ladakh,
India

Aboriginal Tribal Bands
Warlpiri and Anmatjera,
Australia

Sioux Medicine Couple
Rosebud, South Dakota,
USA

Miss Lucy and Miss Harriet
Orroroo,
Australia

Three Generations of Apache
Arizona,
USA

Father and Son
Ollantaytambo,
Peru

Tibetan Buddhist Family
Ladakh,
India

The Chase Family
Vermont,
USA

Sampling Home Brew
Ollantaytambo,
Peru

The Poddyappuhamy Family
At Their Jungle Store,
Sri Lanka

Eloise Chicoine
Albany, Vermont,
USA

Leonard and Rittie Webb
Scaly Mountain, North Carolina,
USA

THE GENERATIONS

Perhaps the most striking difference between my own culture and those I have been privileged to visit in Third World countries is the respect and veneration which is afforded to elders there. Madison Avenue advertising has all but discarded elders as an important segment of our society. And yet in other cultures, like the Australian Aborigines, the Inuits of Canada, and the Maoris of New Zealand, the elderly provide strength, wisdom and stability to the entire culture.

In my travels, I have witnessed time and time again households where venerable grandparents are considered the heads of the extended family, where older women of the clan prepare the young girls for their rites of passage to adulthood, and where older men take the responsibility for teaching not only the most prudent and economical way to perform a task, but also the one most environmentally sound.

The homage to elders in Third World countries is not a new phenomenon. It has been the backbone of all the great cultures and civilizations from time immemorial. Regretably, Third World cultures often seek to emulate First World cultures, and now, in less than a generation, the family's structure and stability throughout the world is radically changing.

Grandmother and Grandson
Isle of Lesvos,
Greece

Grandma and Robbie
Vermont,
USA

Chippewa Sweat Ceremony
North Dakota,
USA

Lester and Gick Taylor
Utah,
USA

Three Generations of Navajo
Canyon de Chelly,
USA

Tinkering on Gramp's Truck
Missouri,
USA

Master and Apprentice
Vermont,
USA

Inuit Family
N.W.T.,
Canada

Pauline and Mr. Christian
Antigua,
West Indies

Fred Sedgwick and Marie
Dentdale,
England

Learning the Ropes
Outer Hebrides,
Scotland

Pack Peddler and Apprentice
Ladakh,
India

Grandmother and Julia
The Dominican Republic

Building the Barn
Chihuahua,
Mexico

Going Out to Milk
Outer Hebrides,
Scotland

Apache Basket Making
Arizona,
USA

The Italian Club of Barre
Vermont,
USA

Coal Miner and Granddaughter
Cerrillos, New Mexico,
USA

Grandfather and Granddaughter
Near Lumle,
Nepal

WORKING

In my travels, notably in Third World countries where life has changed very little, I have happily witnessed people at work, especially the older generations. There is a grace with which elders labor, a rhythm and tempo, an acceptance to be in the here and now with the activity. Whether it be a Mayan elder working at carving out a dugout canoe, a Maori digging a giant pit for a festival cookout, or perhaps a Quechua Indian on the high slopes of the Andes gathering potatoes, elders seem to have the right energy to labor. Energy comes from two Greek root words — en ergos — which mean, in one's work. When you are in your work, you have energy.

Perhaps in our mad dash to embrace the materialistic world, younger generations have not been shown the joys and benefits of working slowly and carefully, mindfully. My adopted Vermont grandfather, Harry Smith, who was perhaps the most beautiful worker I have ever seen, used to encourage me to use a tool, a scythe, for instance, with a precision and grace that his generation knew would make the work go easier. "Breathe into the tool," he would tell us, "and put your whole attention into the job." We would follow his instructions to the letter, with the old man looking on with the eyes of a Zen master, and the tall shimmering grassses would fall with precision.

Lewis Williams, Shearing
Llanfachreth,
Wales

Delia Diaz, Teacher
The Dominican Republic

Grinding Arica Nuts
Sri Lanka

Bright Shining Woman
Canyon de Chelly,
USA

Luisa Lucero, Prairie Midwife
New Mexico,
USA

Susannah Henry
Antigua,
West Indies

Captain Festus Hutchinson
Union Island,
West Indies

Henry Hadlakey
Kansas,
USA

Arthur Roberts
On the Sheep Gather,
Wales

Laura Kermen, Papago
Arizona,
USA

Papago Making Fence
Arizona,
USA

Theron Boyd, Farmer
Vermont,
USA

The Oldest Goodyear Tire Dealer
Nebraska,
USA

Spinning Yak Wool
Nepal

Flujensia Tesecun, Mayan
Guatemala

Parching Corn in the Bush
Union Island,
West Indies

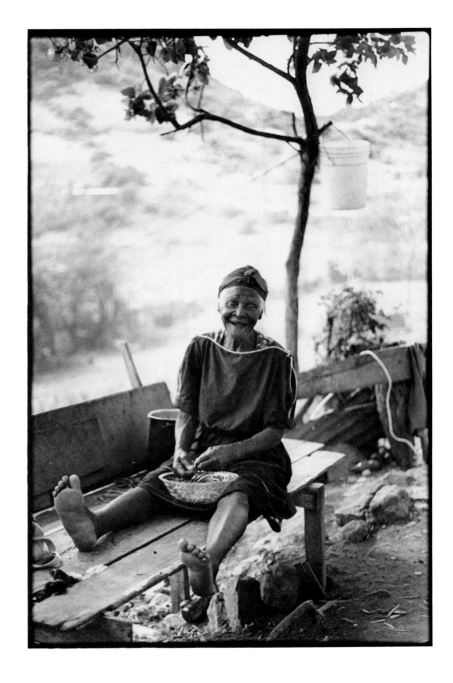

Mistress Margaret Ovid
Union Island,
West Indies

Eighty Year-Old Irrigator
Ambepossa Village,
Sri Lanka

The Hermit With Honeycomb
Appalachian Mountains, Georgia,
USA

LEISURE

Most elders I have photographed do not have television. Nor do they have electricity. Very few have the use of a telephone. And most do not have a car. Making an excursion to a mall for idle shopping or going out to a restaurant for dinner is simply not one of their options. "Then what do they do for fun in their leisure time?" younger generations from my own culture ask me, implying that without modern conveniences and entertainment life is boring and uneventful. I tell them that most elders in underdeveloped countries like Sri Lanka or Nepal or the Dominican Republic show a delight and ease in "just being." Sitting on a porch and watching the sunlight drift in and out of a forest, enjoying the sound of the wind in the trees, or perhaps visiting with a friend uninterrupted for long hours is enough. Enough is actually not the right word. It is more like "perfectly enough."

This is why I am attracted to elders from underdeveloped countries; they have the ability to "just be." That life is enough, just as it is, is their key to happiness.

Without hundreds of choices to confuse them, and with a lifetime of experiences to draw from, these elders still know the secret of good living, that the simple pleasures are the best pleasures.

Abbie and Fred Metcalf
Norwich, Vermont,
USA

Art Storley, Retired Railroader
North Dakota,
USA

Katie and Paloma
"On the Road" in Wyoming,
USA

Where She Was Born
North Dakota,
USA

Flora Johnston's Shell Bus
Outer Hebrides,
Scotland

Mistress Olive Clauden
Union Island,
West Indies

Serenading His Girlfriend
Union Island,
West Indies

The Sea Captain and the Boy
Outer Hebrides,
Scotland

At Glen's Birthday
Vermont,
USA

Ten Year Reunion
Outer Hebrides,
Scotland

The Ed Larkin Contra Dancers
Vermont,
USA

Lemondrop in April Sunshine
North Dakota,
USA

Two Singing Cowboys
Colorado,
USA

Navajo Weaving Lesson
Arizona,
USA

The Silvas at Home
San Miguel de Allende,
Mexico

Harry and Linda
Vermont,
USA

Hughie Jones, Joiner
Wales

One Hundred-Six Year-Old Farmer
Farafra Oasis,
Egypt

Erdine Gonyaw
Glover, Vermont,
USA

WITH ANIMALS

In my travels, I have noticed that elders are more prone to treat animals with kindness and respect than younger generations. Perhaps by the time people become old they have developed a love and an empathy for animals, especially for the suffering which animals must certainly endure: tired bones, aching muscles, and the loss of the vitality of youth.

In Sri Lanka, for example, I once witnessed an old man with a lifelong friend — an elephant — working at moving huge logs in the dense rainforest. The man and the elephant worked beautifully together day after day. There was a mutual respect between the two, as if they both understood that they would starve if there was not a strong communication between them.

In my own home state of Vermont, I always enjoyed seeing an old Vermont logger by the name of Chet Grimes feeding and caring for his sweaty work horses on bitterly cold January afternoons well before he took time to see to his own needs. "Heck, if you don't take care of your hoss's, they won't take care of you."

Chuck Choin, Irrigator
Westcliff, Colorado,
USA

Ann Burke
Vermont,
USA

Old Tomba and His Cat
Near Pokhara,
Nepal

Ed Couch and Josaphine
Mississippi,
USA

Angus MacCormick and the Pup
Outer Hebrides,
Scotland

Mary Teuscher's Pet Pig
California,
USA

Kathy MacClellan and Pet Sheep
Outer Hebrides,
Scotland

In From the Fields
Lesvos,
Greece

Arthur Roberts
Gathering Up the Sheep,
Wales

The Last Herdsman of the Village
Outer Hebrides,
Scotland

Cy McCoy and His Team
Vermont,
USA

Miss Harriet Shephard, Rancher
North Petersburg,
Australia

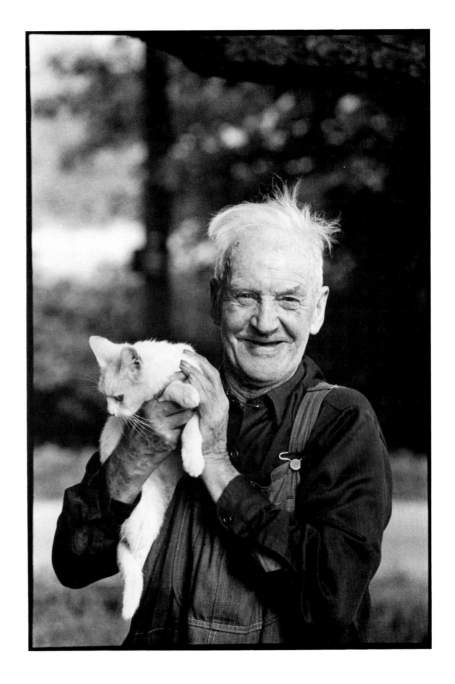

Harry Smith and Zip-Zip
Vermont,
USA

Percy Tollof, Farmer
Near Warkworth,
New Zealand

Donald MacCormick, Crofter
Outer Hebrides,
Scotland

Chet Grimes, Logger
Vermont,
USA

Mr. David Lincoln
Antigua,
West Indies

The Sea Captain and Cheeky
The Outer Hebrides,
Scotland

Ruth Fair
Milking in the Woods, Vermont,
USA

SPIRITUALITY

Gandhi once said that there are as many different religions as there are numbers of people in the world. In my own travels, I have witnessed different cultures performing rites and rituals in their homes and in village shrines: Navajos, Maoris, Incas, Australian Aborigines, Tibetan Buddhists, Papagos, Sufis, Hindus, Christians, and Inuits.

Equally fascinating has been watching elders in different cultures who profess no religion at all and yet exhibit so many of the criteria major religions expound as necessary for living a fulfilling life. Harry Smith, who certainly had never been to church before in all his 83 years, once laughed when I said that I was looking for God. "Well," he said, gently lifting his favorite cat Zip-Zip off the ground and putting her softly against his cheek, "I ain't never lost Him."

Another elder I admired was a Native American from the mountains of southern Colorado. He told me that his religion was simply "placing one moccasin in front of the other with as much mindfulness as I can muster."

Poet Laureat, Maya Angelou, said it even more succinctly when she read her inauguration poem for President Bill Clinton in January, 1993. "Wake up in the morning and simply say (to the rock, tree, our planet) Good Morning."

Saint Gaspar's Day
Above Ollantaytambo,
Peru

Tibetan Buddhist Praying
Near Manang,
Nepal

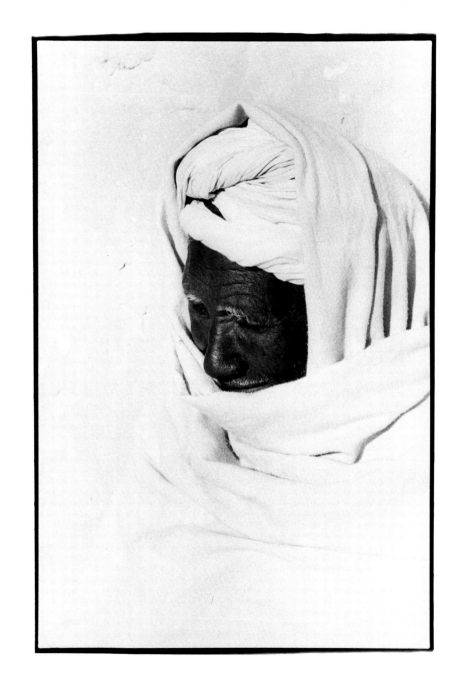

Sufi at the Oasis
Farafra,
Egypt

Old Deschini, Navajo Shaman
Canyon de Chelly,
USA

Wally Fayant, Tramp
Crossing Nevada,
USA

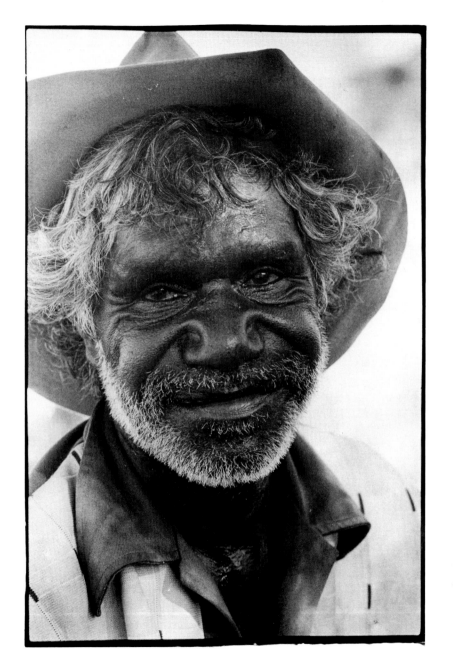

Louis Paga, Warlpiri
Outside Alice Springs,
Australia

Margaret Ovid at Church
Union Island,
West Indies

The Last Great Incan Shaman
Outside Cuzco,
Peru

Laura Kermen at Prayer
Papago Indian Reservation,
USA

High Andean Farmer
Ollantaytambo,
Peru

Tibetan Buddhist Grandmother
Ladakh,
India

Old Nino, Maori
North Island,
New Zealand

Sadhu on Pilgrimage
Near Manang,
Nepal

Blind Gospel Singer
Virginia,
USA

Alpheus Ryan, The Baptiser
Union Island,
West Indies

Inuit Prayer Ceremony
Whale Cove, N.W.T.,
Canada